Peter Köhler · Alciro Theodoro da Silva

GÖTTINGEN

Medien-Verlag Schubert

ISBN 978-3-929229-71-4

Vorwort

„Göttingen ist eine kleine Stadt, durch die aber die Ströme der Welt gehen." Dieser Satz, den Bundespräsident Theodor Heuss 1951 ins Goldene Buch eintrug, beschreibt bis heute Göttingens außergewöhnliche Stellung: als weltoffene Stadt in der Provinz, als Ort von Altstadtromantik und moderner Wissenschaft. Auf einer Urkunde Ottos des Großen erstmals erwähnt, ist Göttingen über tausend Jahre alt. Das Rathaus und die mächtigen Kirchen, zahlreiche alte Straßenzüge und manche reich geschmückten Fachwerkhäuser zeugen von der mittelalterlichen Vergangenheit, als die Tuchmacherstadt Göttingen bis ins Baltikum bekannt war. Heute erstrahlt Göttingens Ruf dank seiner Universität sogar weltweit; über 40 Nobelpreisträger lebten, lernten und lehrten hier. Die Universität prägt das geistige Leben der Stadt, ihre offene und internationale Atmosphäre. Heute zählt Göttingen 130 000 Einwohner und bewahrt auch als moderne Großstadt in der Mitte Deutschlands und Europas seinen Charakter: in der Tradition verwurzelt und der Welt zugewandt zu sein.

Preface

"Göttingen is a small town through which, however, the streams of the world flow." This sentence, entered into the Golden Book by President Theodor Heuss in 1951, still describes Göttingen's unusual position today: as a cosmopolitan yet provincial town, a place of old world charm and modern science. First mentioned in a document of Otto the Great, Göttingen is over a thousand years old. The Town Hall and the great churches, countless old streets and many richly decorated half-timbered houses bear witness to its medieval past. Back then, the city was renowned all the way to the Baltic for its textile industry.

These days Göttingen's reputation is internationally known, thanks to its university – over 40 Nobel Prize winners have lived, learned and taught here. The university influences the spiritual life of the city, its open and international atmosphere. Today Göttingen's population is 130.000 and the city has retained its character, even as a modern town in the middle of Germany and Europe it remains rooted in traditions and open to the world.

Tradition und Moderne, Zweckdenken und Kunststreben existieren in Göttingen nebeneinander: Vor dem modernen Neuen Rathaus von 1978 und flankiert vom klassizistischen Amtshaus aus dem Jahr 1835 reitet der Doppelkentaur, eine von Uwe Appold aus Flensburg 1987 als Torso geschaffene Eisenkriegerskulptur.

The traditional and the modern, the functional and the artistic: they exist side by side in Göttingen. In front of the modern New Town Hall of 1978 and flanked by the classic administrative building of the "Amtshaus" of 1835, rides a double centaur, an iron warrior sculpture created as a torso by Uwe Appold from Flensburg in 1987.

Die Albanikirche war der geistliche Mittelpunkt des erstmals 953 urkundlich erwähnten, am westlichen Hang des Hainbergs gelegenen Dorfes Gutingi, dem die spätere, im Leinetal erfolgte Neu- und Stadtgründung ihren Namen verdankt. Der Legende nach hatte der Germanen-Missionar Bonifatius genau 200 Jahre zuvor hier eine erste Kirche errichtet und dem heiligen Albanus geweiht. Ihre heutige Gestalt erhielt die Kirche im 15. Jahrhundert.

St. Albani Church was the spiritual centre of the village Gutingi, first documented in 953, on the western slope of Hainberg. The newly founded town in the Leine valley owes its name to that village. According to legend, the Teutonic missionary Bonifatius had erected the first church here exactly 200 years earlier and consecrated it to the saint Albanus. The church got its current form in the 15th century.

Blick auf die Göttinger Altstadt vom Nordturm der Johanniskirche. In der Bildmitte ragt der Turm der Jacobikirche aus dem Häusermeer empor. Im Zweiten Weltkrieg nahezu unzerstört und in den 60er- und 70er- Jahren im Geist der Zeit modernisiert, spannt Göttingens Zentrum den Bogen vom 13. Jahrhundert bis in die unmittelbare Gegenwart.

A view of Göttingen's old city from the northern spire of the Church of St. Johannis. In the middle of the picture St. Jakobi Church's spire rises above the sea of houses. Nearly undamaged in the Second World War and modernised in the spirit of the times in the Sixties and Seventies, Göttingen's centre spans the 13th century until present day.

Die Dorntze im Alten Rathaus war der Sitzungssaal des städtischen Rates, der hier vom Mittelalter bis in die jüngere Vergangenheit tagte. Durch Öffnungen im Fußboden wurde sie von dem darunter liegenden Raum beheizt. Das Spitzbogenfenster wurde Anfang des 20. Jahrhunderts ausgemalt: Um den Brunnen des Lebens gruppieren sich die allegorischen Gestalten von Handel, Handwerk, Landwirtschaft, Wissenschaft und Kunst - ein Sinnbild Göttinger Bürgerstolzes auf Gewerbefleiß und geistigen Fortschritt.

The "Dorntze" in the Old Town Hall was the historical meeting place of the town council, which met here from the Middle Ages until the recent past. It was heated from the room below through openings in the floor. The pointed arch window was painted at the beginning of the 20th century: grouped around the fountain of life the allegorical figures of Trade, Craft, Agriculture, Science and Art are a symbol of Göttingen's pride in its busy trade and spiritual progress.

M ittelpunkt des städtischen Lebens und täglicher Treffpunkt für Jung und Alt ist seit alters der Marktplatz vor dem Alten Rathaus. Bis heute zeugt das massive, einer Burg ähnelnde Bauwerk des 15. Jahrhunderts mit seinem Zinnenkranz und den vorkragenden Ecktürmchen von der Wehrhaftigkeit der mittelalterlichen Stadt, während die Cafés rund um den Platz von moderner Lebensart künden.

T he market square in front of the Old Town Hall has always been the centre of the town's life and a daily meeting place for young and old alike. Even today, the massive fortress-like 15th century building with its pewter wreath and overhanging corner towers defends the medieval town, whilst the cafes around the square show a modern lifestyle.

Heute kommt man nur mehr freiwillig hinein, im Rahmen einer Stadtführung: Zwischen 1580 und 1620 indes dienten die Seitengewölbe unterhalb der Dorntze als Stadtgefängnis. Einer der Inhaftierten war ein gewisser Hans Hacken, der 1581 in den Reinsborn gepinkelt hatte. Was heute allenfalls wie grober Unfug wirkt, war damals ein ernstes Delikt, das die Wasserversorgung der Stadt gefährdete.

Today people only end up here voluntarily, as part of a city tour: Between 1580 and 1620 the vaults under the Dorntze served as the town's prison. One of the prisoners, a certain Hans Hacken, had urinated into the Reinsborn. What today would count as a misdemeanour, was then a real crime, as it threatened the town's water supply.

Aus dem Nebel der Geschichte ragen sie in die Gegenwart: Die Kommende der Deutschordensritter - also das Hauptgebäude ihres Wirtschaftshofes - und die Marienkirche. Beide wurden Anfang des 14. Jahrhunderts errichtet und sind die ältesten Monumente der so genannten Neustadt westlich der Alten Leine, des heutigen Leinekanals. Beide Gebäude liegen an der Groner-Tor-Straße.

They move out of the fog of history into the present: The command of the Knights of the German Order – in other words the headquarters of their business – and St. Marien Church. Both were built in the 14th century and are the oldest monuments of the so-called New Town to thewest of the Old Leine, today the Leine Canal. Both buildings lie on Groner Tor Street.

Blick von der Johannisstraße zu Göttingens mäch-
tiger Hauptkirche, der Johanniskirche mit dem
markanten Doppelturm. Auf dem Nordturm (links)
versah der Türmer von 1412 bis 1921 seinen Wachdienst.
Danach wurde die Wächterstube 80 Jahre lang als
„Deutschlands höchste Studentenbude" von der Theologischen Fakultät der Universität mietfrei vergeben.
Heute dient sie als Kapelle.

A view from Johannis Street to Göttingen's mighty
main church, the Church of St. Johannis with its
cha-racteristic twin spires. The tower guard did his duty
on the northern spire (left) from 1412 to 1921. After that
the guard rooms are given as rent-free rooms for 80 years
by the university's Theology Faculty – "Germany's high-
est student digs". Today it´s used as a chapel.

Ernste Gesichter und Fratzen schmücken das 1897 errichtete Eckhaus Theaterstraße/Jüdenstraße des Bäckermeisters, streitbaren Kommunalpolitikers und humoristischen Heimatschriftstellers Ernst Honig (1861 bis 1930), der hier wohl auch sich selbst in Stein hat hauen lassen. Er schuf die populäre Figur des „Schorse Szültenbürger", die den Typ des behäbigen Göttinger Kleinbürgers parodierte. Seine Geschichten schrieb Ernst Honig meist im Missingsch, einer Sprachform zwischen Hochdeutsch und Platt. Von ihm stammt der „Chöttingensche" Wahlspruch: „Ne chute chebratene Chans is 'ne chute Chabe Chottes!"

Serious faces and grimaces decorate the 1897 erected house on the corner of Theatre and Jüden Streets. It belonged to the master baker, confrontational community politician and humorous "Heimat" author Ernst Honig (1861–1930), who apparently had himself hewn in stone here. He created the popular figure of "Schorse Szültenbürger", a parody of the portly Göttinger burgher type. Ernst Honig wrote his stories mostly in Missingsch, a language between High and Low German. He is the source of the Göttingen motto: "A good roasted goose is a gift from God!"

Vom Wohlstand und künstlerischen Geschmack Göttinger Bürger im 16. Jahrhundert zeugt die Fassade des 1549 errichteten Hovetschen oder, nach einem späteren Besitzer, Schröderschen Hauses in der Weender Straße. In ihrem reichen Figurenschmuck hat der Bauherr und Tuchmacher Jürgen Hovet neben Fabelwesen, Heiligen und Engeln auch seinen Beruf in Gestalt eines Weberschiffchens verewigt sowie sich selbst und seine Familie porträtiert.

The Hovetschen house on Weender Street or, as it was then named after a later owner, the Schrödersche house was built in 1549. Its façade bears witness to the wealth and artistic taste of the Göttinger citizens in the 16th century. Beside the richly decorated figures of mythical creatures, saints and angels, the owner and textile manufacturer Jürgen Hovet has immortalized his profession, in the form of a shuttle, as well as himself and his family.

Üppig verziert mit Rankenwerk, Grotesken, biblischen Szenen, Wappen und Bürgerbildnissen ist die Renaissance-Fassade der vom kunstsinnigen Bürgermeister Gyseler Swanenflogel 1547 - 1549 umgebauten Junkernschänke an der Kreuzung Barfüßerstraße/Jüdenstraße.

This Renaissance façade, opulently decorated with vines, grotesques, biblical scenes, coats of arms and civic scenes, can be found on the Junkernschänke on the intersection of Barfüßer Street and Jüden Street. It was rebuilt by the artistic mayor Gyseler Swanenflogel 1547 – 1549.

Abendstimmung bei der Michaeliskirche in der Kurzen Straße. Die Kirche wurde 1789 als erste katholische Kirche der Stadt geweiht, nachdem bereits 1747 der katholische Gottesdienst im lutherischen Göttingen wieder zugelassen worden war. Diese damals ungewöhnliche Liberalität in Glaubensdingen hatte den Zweck, Gelehrte und Studenten auch aus den nicht-lutherischen Ländern anzuziehen.

Twilight mood at St. Michaelis church in Kurzen Street. The church was first consecrated in 1789 as the town's first Catholic church, after Catholic church services had been allowed again in Lutheran Göttingen after 1747. This religious liberty was unusual for the times but had the aim of attracting academics and students also from non-Lutheran countries.

Blick über die Weender Straße zum 74 Meter hohen Turm der Jacobikirche, der Legende zufolge eine Stiftung Heinrichs des Löwen. Die meisten Häuser an dieser Stelle der Weender stammen aus den Jahren von 1750 bis Anfang des 19. Jahrhunderts. Die Weender Straße selbst ist als Geschäftsstraße wie als Flaniermeile die historische Schlagader der Stadt.

A view over Weender Street to the 74-metre high spire of St. Jakobi church, according to legend a gift from Henry the Lion. Most of the houses in this part of Weender date back to the time from 1750 till the beginning of the 19th century. Weender Street itself is the town's historical artery - for commercial business as well as leisurely strollers.

In der überraschenden Farbenpracht von 1480 erstrahlt das hohe gotische Kirchenschiff der Jakobikirche. Noch älter ist der von einem unbekannten Meister 1402 geschaffene Wandelaltar, der Szenen aus dem Leben Jesu sowie des Namenspatrons und Apostels Jakobus des Älteren zeigt.

The high Gothic nave of St. Jakobi church shines in surprising colours of 1480. The moveable altar, made by an unknown master in 1402, is even older. It shows scenes from Jesus' life as well as its namesake, the apostle Jakob the Elder.

Göttingens anmutiges Wahrzeichen: das Gänselie-sel. Seit 1901 schmückt die Gänsemädchenfigur den Brunnen vor dem Alten Rathaus. Die Jugendstil-Skulptur, entworfen vom Berliner Architekten Heinrich Stöckhardt und geschaffen vom Charlottenburger Bildhauer Paul Nisse, stellt eine jedermann vertraute Wochenmarktszene dar und wurde schnell populär. Schon 1927 verwendete die Stadt das Gänseliesel in einer Werbeaktion.

Göttingen's lovely trademark: "Gänseliesel". The statue of the goose girl has decorated the fountain in front of the Old Town hall since 1901. The Art Nouveau sculpture, created by the Berlin architect Heinrich Stöckhardt and made by the Charlottenburger sculptor Paul Nisse, depicts a weekly market scene that everyone is familiar with. It quickly became popular. As far back as 1927 the town used Gänseliesel in a marketing campaign.

Das meistgeküsste Mädchen der Welt ist das Gänseliesel. Bald nach Aufstellung der lieblichen Figur bürgerte es sich ein, dass die neuimmatrikulierten Studenten ihr einen Kuss aufdrückten. Heute, im Zeitalter der Massenuniversität, gehört es zur schönen Pflicht der Doktoranden, nach bestandenem Rigorosum dem Mädchen Blumen zu bringen und ein Bussi zu geben. So schlägt das hübsche Gänse-Girl die Brücke von Göttingens ackerbürgerlicher Vergangenheit zur akademischen Gegenwart.

Gänseliesel is the most-kissed girl in the world. Soon after the lovely figure was set up it became traditional for newly registered students to give her a kiss. Today, in the times of the mass university, it is the enjoyable duty of PhD students to bring the girl flowers and a kiss after they have passed their rigours. So the pretty goose girl has bridged the gap from Göttingen's agricultural past to its academic present.

Als älteste Straßenhändlerin der Welt ins Guiness-buch der Rekorde eingetragen wurde Johanna Wilhelmine Charlotte Müller (1840-1935). Von 1889 bis zu ihrem Tod saß sie bei Wind und Wetter auf dem Bahnhofsplatz und verkaufte Obst und Süßigkeiten. An sie erinnert vor dem Bahnhof die Büste von Katharine Hobson-Kraus, die Charlotte Müller noch zu ihren Lebzeiten modellierte.

Johanna Wilhelmine Charlotte Müller (1840–1935) has made it into the Guinness Book of World Records as the oldest street seller in the world. From 1889 until her death she sat on the railway station's square in wind and weather and sold fruit and sweets. A bust in front of the station commemorates her. It was modelled in her lifetime by Katharine Hobson-Kraus.

Georg Christoph Lichtenberg (1742-1799), Physiker von Beruf, Schriftsteller aus Passion und Wahlgöttinger seit 1763, ist einer der großen deutschen Autoren des 19. Jahrhunderts. Seine erst postum veröffentlichten „Sudelbücher" weisen ihn als scharfen Beobachter, originellen Denker und witzigen Skeptiker aus. Das von Volker Neuhoff aus Nienburg geschaffene Bronzedenkmal ist seit 1992 Mittelpunkt des Akademiehofes der alten Universitätsbibliothek am Papendiek. Die Bronze stammt von eingeschmolzenen Lenin- und Enver-Hodscha-Denkmälern aus Albanien.

Georg Christoph Lichtenberg (1742–1799), a physician by profession and an author from passion, citizen of Göttingen by choice since 1763, is one of the great German authors of the 19th century. His "Sudelbücher" books, published posthumously, showed him to be a keen observer, original thinker and witty sceptic. The bronze sculpture created by Volker Neuhoff from Nienburg has been the centre of the academic court of the old university library on Papendiek since 1992. The bronze stems from molten Lenin and Enver-Hodscha monuments from Albania.

Einer der großen Göttinger Baumeister war Christian Friedrich Andreas Rohns (1787-1853). Sein Grabmal liegt in Sichtweite des nach antikem Vorbild gestalteten Badehauses, das Rohns 1820 errichtete. 1972 wegen Baufälligkeit abgerissen, wurde das achteckige Gebäude originalgetreu rekonstruiert und dient seither einem Antiquitätengeschäft als Ausstellungsgebäude.

Christian Friedrich Andreas Rohns (1787–1853) was one of the great Göttinger master builders. Rohns tomb lies in view of the bath house, which he built according to an antique example in 1820. Torn down in 1972 because of dilapidation, the octagonal building was reconstructed true to the original and has since served an antique store as exhibition room.

Der Hiroshimaplatz mit dem klassizistischen Amtshaus von 1835. Im Hintergrund der Turm des Neuen Rathauses von 1978. Das Amtshaus diente bis 1945 als Kaserne. Als solche war es 110 Jahre zuvor errichtet worden, weil bis dahin die meisten Soldaten der Göttinger Garnison in Privatunterkünften wohnten - und mit den Bürgern fraternisierten: Gegen die Göttinger Revolution von 1831 war die Obrigkeit deshalb machtlos.

Hiroshima square with the classic 1835 "Amtshaus". In the background – the tower of the New Town Hall of 1978. The "Amtshaus" served as a barracks until 1945. It had been built as such 110 years before, because most soldiers in Göttingen's garrison had previously lived in private homes and fraternised with the civilians. Therefore the authorities were powerless against the Göttinger Revolution of 1831.

Die vom Mathematiker und Astronomen Carl Friedrich Gauß berechnete Bahn des Kleinplaneten Ceres durch die Sternbilder von Stier und Jungfrau wird auf dem Zuckerhutdach des originellen Verkehrsbüros auf dem Bahnhofplatz nachgezeichnet. Dank dieser Berechnung konnte die von Giuseppe Piazzi am 1.1.1801 entdeckte, aber verloren gegangene Ceres Ende des Jahres am Sternenhimmel wiedergefunden werden.

The path of the small planet Ceres through the star signs Taurus and Virgo, as calculated by the mathematician and astronomer Carl Friedrich Gauß, has been laid out on the sugarloaf roof of the original travel agency on the station square. Thanks to this calculation, the lost planet Ceres, discovered by Giuseppe Piazzi on 1.1.1801, was found again in the sky at the end of the year.

Ein Wahrzeichen der Georg-August-Universität ist das Aulage-gebäude am Wilhelmsplatz. 1837, zum hundertsten Geburtstag der Göttinger Alma mater, wurde es errichtet. Hier hat die Universitätsleitung ihren Sitz, tagt die Akademie der Wissenschaften - und hier befindet sich auch der historische Karzer, das Universitätsgefängnis.

A landmark of the George Augustus University is the auditorium building on Wilhelm square. It was built in 1837 on the occasion of the hundredth birthday of the Göttinger alma mater. It is the seat of the university management and the academy of sciences meets here – and the historical "Karzer", the university's prison, can also be found here.

Der Karzer im Aulagebäude der Universität. Die Haft von einem bis zu 14 Tagen wurde vom Rektor verhängt. Die Palette der Vergehen war lang: Trunkenheit, Glücksspiel, nächtlicher Lärm, Halten gefährlicher Hunde, Beleidigung oder Faulheit waren einige davon. Schon Ende des 19. Jahrhunderts hatten die Studenten die Einkerkerung weniger als Strafe denn als Abwechslung empfunden: Im Karzer gesessen zu haben, gehörte zum guten Ton. 1933 wurde das spartanisch eingerichtete „Hotel zur akademischen Freiheit" stillgelegt.

The "Karzer" in the university's auditorium building. Sentences of one to 14 days were passed by the rector. The list of offences was long: drunkenness, gambling, night-time noise, owning a dangerous dog, offensive behaviour or laziness to name a few. Already at the end of the 19th century the students considered these sentences less of a punishment than a change. Sitting in the "Karzer" was the done thing. In 1933 the "Hotel to Academic Freedom", with its Spartan furnishings, was closed down.

Das „Bismarckhäuschen" genannte Bollwerk von 1447 blieb als einziges nach dem Schleifen der Stadtmauer im 18. Jahrhundert erhalten. 1833 bezog der Jurastudent Otto von Bismarck den Wehrturm - eher unfreiwillig: Der Magistrat hatte dem Raubein den Aufenthalt in der Stadt außer zum Vorlesungsbesuch verboten. Dreimal, insgesamt 17 Tage, hatte der nachmalige Reichskanzler im Karzer eingesessen.

The 1447 bulwark known as "Bismarck House" was the only one left standing when the town walls were torn down in the 18th century. In 1833 the law student Otto von Bismarck moved into the fortress – rather involuntarily. The magistrate had forbidden the "rough diamond" from staying in the town other than to go to lectures. The chancellor-to-be was locked in the "Karzer" three times, for a total of 17 days.

Eine Kirche war die Keimzelle der Universität: Nachdem Georg August, in Personalunion König von Großbritannien und Kurfürst von Hannover, 1733 die Universität gestiftet hatte, wurde das einstige Dominikanerkloster zwischen Papendiek und Paulinerstraße zu ihrem Sitz bestimmt und für die Zwecke der Hochschule umgebaut. Die gotische Klosterkirche St. Peter und Paul diente zuerst als Gotteshaus und Versammlungssaal für die Universitätsangehörigen, später als Auditorium und Katalogsaal. Heute bildet die restaurierte Paulinerkirche einen würdigen Rahmen für Ausstellungen und Vorträge.

The church was the seed of the university. After George Augustus, king of Great Britain and elector of Hannover in one person, donated the university in 1733, the former Dominican monastery between Papendiek and Pauliner street was chosen as its seat and renovated as a college. The Gothic monastery church St. Peter and Paul served first as a house of God and as a meeting place for university employees, later as an auditorium and catalogue hall. Today the restored Pauliner church is a dignified location for exhibitions and lectures.

Den Physiker Wilhelm Weber (stehend; 1804-1891) und den Mathematiker und Astronomen Carl Friedrich Gauß (1777-1855), die 1833 den elektromagnetischen Telegraphen erfunden hatten, zeigt das von Ferdinand Hartzer 1899 geschaffene Denkmal ins wissenschaftliche Gespräch vertieft. Der Göttinger Volksmund behauptet allerdings, Weber sage gerade zu Gauß: „Carl, lass mich auch mal sitzen!"

The physicist Wilhelm Weber (standing, 1804–1891) and the mathematician and astronomer Carl Friedrich Gauß (1777–1855). They invented the electromagnetic telegraph in 1833. The memorial, created by Ferdinand Hartzer in 1899, shows the two absorbed in scientific conversation. In Göttingen there is a standing joke that Weber is saying to Gauß: "Carl, let me sit down for once!"

Die 1816 im antikisierenden Stil fertiggestellte Sternwarte. Ihr erster Direktor war Carl Friedrich Gauß. Von 1901 bis 1909 amtierte hier Karl Schwarzschild, der Begründer der Astrophysik und Entdecker des den Fotografen vertrauten „Schwarzschildeffekts" bei Langzeitbelichtungen. Heute, da die Sternwarte nicht mehr dem astronomischen Standard gerecht wird, dient sie als Seminargebäude und als Museum, in dem wissenschaftliche Geräte und Erinnerungs-stücke an Gauß ausgestellt sind.

The observatory was built in an antique style and completed in 1816. Its first director was Carl Friedrich Gauß. From 1901 to 1909 Karl Schwarzschild was in office. He was the founder of astro-physics and discovered the "Schwarzschild effect" with long exposure times, well-known among photographers. These days the observatory no longer does justice to the astronomical standard. Instead it serves as a seminar building and museum, in which scientific equipment and Gauß memorabilia are on show.

Weithin sichtbares Wahrzeichen der modernen Georg-August-Universität ist ihr Mehrzweckgebäude, der sogenannte „Blaue Turm", der das 1968 - 1972 errichtete geisteswissenschaftliche Zentrum überragt und nach seinen blau eloxierten Fensterscheiben benannt ist.

The multi-purpose building known as the "Blue Tower", a landmark of the modern George Augustus University that can be seen from afar. It towers above the arts centre, built 1968 – 1972 and named for its blue anodized window panes.

Blick über den Campus des geisteswissenschaftlichen Zentrums der Universität zur Eingangsrotunde der neuen Universitätsbibliothek. Hier, am Platz der Göttinger Sieben, wo Juristen, Ökonomen, Sozialwissenschaftler, Philologen und Theologen ihre Institute haben und sich Zentralmensa und Zentrales Hörsaalgebäude befinden, schlägt das Herz der modernen Universität.

A view over the campus of the arts centre to the entrance rotunda of the new university library. Here, on the square of the Göttinger Seven, where jurists, economists, social scientists, philologists and theologians have their institutes and where the central canteen and the central auditorium are located, beats the heart of the university.

Der 1992 fertiggestellte Neubau der Niedersächsischen Staats- und Universitätsbibliothek am Platz der Göttinger Sieben. Das Gebäude ähnelt einer Hand, die vom Hauptblock am Universitätsforum im Norden aus fünf fingerähnliche Pavillons nach Süden ausstreckt.

The new building of Lower Saxony's state and university library on the square of the Göttinger Seven was completed in 1992. The building looks like a hand, its main block on the university forum in the north, with five finger-like pavilions that stretch out to the south.

Hohe Spannung und sublimen Kunstgenuss bieten jedes Jahr die Göttinger Händel-Festspiele, auf denen Künstler von internationalem Ruf die Opern, Oratorien und Kantaten des großen Barockkomponisten Georg Friedrich Händel aufführen. Ihren Ursprung haben die Festspiele im Jahr 1920, als die Akademische Orchestervereinigung unter Leitung des Kunsthistorikers Oskar Hagen die Oper „Rodelinde" von 1725 zu Gehör brachte, die erste Aufführung einer Händel-Oper nach dessen Tod.

Göttingen's Handel Festival brings suspense and sublime art enjoyment every year. Internationally acclaimed artists perform the operas, oratorios and cantatas of the great Baroque composer George Friedrich Handel. The festival started in the year 1920, when the academic united orchestra, under the direction of the art historian Oskar Hagen, performed the 1725 opera "Rodelinde". It was the first performance of a Handel opera after his death.

Spannung und Dramatik, künstlerisch verfremdet: das Deutsche Theater. 1890 im Stil der Neorenaissance errichtet, erwarb sich das Haus unter dem Intendanten Heinz Hilpert, der von 1950 bis 1966 amtierte, einen bundesweiten Ruf. Hilpert hatte zuvor in Berlin das Deutsche Theater geleitet und brachte von dort den programmatischen Namen mit.

Suspense and drama, artistically alienated: the German Theatre. Built in 1890 in the Neorenaissance style, the house achieved an international reputation under the director Heinz Hilpert, who was in office from 1950 to 1966. Hilpert had previously directed the German Theatre in Berlin and brought its leading name with him.

An die Ackerbürgervergangenheit Göttingens erinnert der 1914 gestiftete Hirtenbrunnen am Groner Tor. Seit dem Mittelalter trieben hier die Hirten die städtischen Kuhherden auf die Weiden im Westen hinaus. Noch 1870 hielt man in Göttingen Vieh im Stadtinnern; dann erst sorgten Industrialisierung und Modernisierung für ein Ende der bäuerlichen Wirtschaft innerhalb der Altstadt und brachten den Viehaustrieb zum Erliegen.

The "Hirtenbrunnen" (Shepherd's fountain) on Groner Gate commemorates Göttingen's agricultural past. It was donated in 1914. In the Middle Ages the shepherds drove the town's cow herds onto the meadows out to the west. As late as 1870 cattle were held in Göttingen's inner city; only then did industrialisation and modernisation see to it that the rustic economy inside the city and the cow herding came to an end.

Ein Blickfang in den Schillerwiesen unterhalb des Hainberges ist der Jérômepavillon, ein Gartenhaus des späten 18. Jahrhunderts. Es stand einst im Westen vor der Stadt und soll Jérôme, als Bruder Napoleons Regent des Königreichs Westphalen und bekannt als „König Lustig", zu galanten Abenteuern gedient haben. 1935 wurde es in den Park umgesetzt. Die Schillerwiesen wurden Anfang des 20. Jahrhunderts nach dem Vorbild der englischen Gartenarchitektur angelegt. Ihren Namen erhielten sie 1905 bei der Feier zu Schillers hundertstem Todestag.

The Jérôme pavilion is an eye-catcher on the Schillerwiesen lawns under the Hainberg. The pavilion is a summerhouse from the late 18th century. It once stood in the west of the city and is said to have served Jérôme during gallant adventures. Jérôme, as Napoleon's brother, ruled of the kingdom Westphalia and known as "King (of) Fun". In 1935 it was moved into the park. The Schillerwiesen were laid out according to English garden architecture at the beginning of the 20th century. It was named in 1905 during a celebration in honour of Schiller, a hundred years after his death.

Ob Ostermarkt, Gänselieselfest oder die „Nacht der Kultur", wenn das Göttinger Symphonieorchester ein Freiluftkonzert gibt, ob Präsentation von Firmen oder Vereinen, politische Kundgebung oder Werbung für einen guten Zweck: Der Marktplatz vor dem Alten Rathaus ist Forum und Schaubühne für vielfältige Aktionen, und auch die Kinder kommen auf ihre Kosten, wenn sie hier bis in den späten Abend Karussell fahren können.

Whether it is the Easter Market, the "Gänselieselfest" or the "Night of Culture", or when Göttingen's symphony orchestra puts on an open-air concert; be it a company or club presentation, a political rally or advertising for a charitable cause: The market square in front of the Old City Hall is a forum and a stage for a wide variety of activities. Even the children get their money's worth when they are able to ride the merry-go-round here late into the night.

Winterabendstimmung am Kiessee, dem Herzstück des in den 50er- Jahren angelegten Landschaftsparks im Südwesten Göttingens. Ob zum Schlittschuhlaufen, Spazierengehen oder sommerlichen Segeln und Bootfahren, das Erholungsgebiet wird das ganze Jahr über viel besucht. In den ersten Jahren, als man noch baden durfte, galt das Gelände sogar als „Lido von Göttingen", weil manche Familie, die sich keine Reise leisten konnte, hier ihren Urlaub verbrachte.

Winter evening atmosphere on the lake Kiessee, at the heart of the park in the southwest of Göttingen, that was laid out in the Fifties. Whether ice skating, going for a walk or sailing and boating in summer, many people visit this recreational area throughout the year. In the first years, when swimming was allowed here, the area was considered the "Lido of Göttingen". It was a place for families who could not afford to travel, to spend their holidays.

Einen Hauch von Ritterburgenromantik verströmt die Burgruine Plesse nördlich Göttingens. Im 11. Jahrhundert erbaut, von wechselnden Herren genutzt, im Dreißigjährigen Krieg von Tilly eingenommen, danach verlassen und dem Verfall preisgegeben, wurde sie im 18. Jahrhundert als Ausflugsziel entdeckt. Ihr weithin sichtbarer Bergfried lockte vor allem Studenten an, die in dieser einst hessischen Enklave vom strengen hannoverschen Reglement befreit waren. Ihren Namen hat die Burg von ihrem Baumaterial, weißem Kalkstein: die Helle, Blasse (= Plesse).

A trace of chivalrous romance exhudes from the fortress ruin Plesse north of Göttingen. Built in the 11th century, ruled by changing lords, taken over by Tilly in the Thirty Years War, then abandoned and left to decay, it was discovered as a tourist attraction in the 18th century. Especially students were attracted to the hillside fortifications, as they were free from the strict regulations of Hanover in this Hessian enclave. The name of the fortress comes from its building material, white limestone: the adjective "Blasse" (= Plesse) means "pale".

Idyllisch liegt das ehemalige Kloster Bursfelde mit seiner romanischen Basilika unterhalb des Bramwaldes im Wesertal. 1093 als Benediktinerabtei gegründet, in der Reformation lutherisch geworden, 1589 endgültig aufgehoben und heute als Tagungs- und Kulturzentrum genutzt, hat sich aus der Klosterzeit der Titel „Abt von Bursfelde" über die Jahrhunderte gehalten: Mit ihm darf sich der Senior der evangelischen theologischen Fakultät in Göttingen schmücken.

The idyllic site of the former monastery Bursfelde, with its Roman basilica below the Bram woods in the Weser valley. It was founded as a Benedictine abbey in 1093 and became Lutheran during the Reformation. In 1589 it was definitively closed and is today used as a cultural and conference centre. It has retained the title "Abbot of Bursfelde" over the centuries. The head of the Protestant Theology Faculty in Göttingen has the right to this title.

Festlich illuminiert sind Göttingens Gassen und Geschäfte zur Adventszeit: Blick vom Sporthaus über den Marktplatz vor dem Alten Rathaus bis zu den Zwillingstürmen der Johanniskirche. Hier, auf dem Marktplatz und dem Johanniskirchhof, findet jedes Jahr der Weihnachtsmarkt statt.

Festively illuminated – Göttingen's streets and shops in the advent season. A view from the Sport house over the market square in front of the Old Town Hall all the way to the twin spires of the Church of St. Johannis. A Christmas market takes place here every year, on the square in front of the Church of St. Johannis.

UNSER VERLAGSPROGRAMM

Hamburg
Alster, die – ein Alltagsmärchen
Altona von A-Z
Barmbek im Wandel
Barmbek von A-Z
Bergedorf, Lohbrügge, Vierlande, Marschlande
Eimsbüttel von A-Z
Eppendorf von A-Z
Feuerwehr-Buch Hamburg, das Große
Hamburg – Stadt der Brücken
Hamburg im Bombenkrieg –1940-1945
Hamburg leuchtet – die Hansestadt zur Blauen Stunde
Hamburgs Neustadt im Wandel
Hamburgs schönste Seiten
Hamburgs Speicherstadt
Hamburgs stolze Fregatten – Konvoi schifffahrt im 17. Jahrhundert
Hamburgs Straßennamen erzählen Geschichte
Harburg – von 1970 bis heute
Harburg von A-Z
Langenhorn im Wandel
Polizei im Einsatz (Video)
Pompöser Leichenzug zur schlichten Grabstäte – ... St. Michaelis
Rothenburgsort, Veddel im Wandel
Winterhude von A-Z

Schleswig-Holstein
Ahrensburg – Stadt mit Adelsprädikat
Bad Oldesloe
Bad Segeberg im Wandel
Eckernförde – Portrait einer Ostseestadt
Fontane in Schleswig-Holstein und Hamburg
Helgoland
Kiels schönste Seiten
Sagenhaftes Sylt
St. Peter-Ording
Sylt – die großen Jahrzehnte – in den 1950er-, 60er-70er-, 80er-Jahren
Sylt – Noch mehr Inselgeschichten
Sylt im Wandel – Menschen, Strand und mehr
Sylt prominent
Sylts schönste Seiten

Niedersachsen
Buchholz in der Nordheide
Buxtehude, Altes Land
Celle – Stadt und Landkreis
Celler Hengstparade, die
Cuxhaven
Cuxhaven – Stadt am Tor zur Welt
Göttingen
Hadeln, Wursten, Kehdingen

Hannovers schönste Seiten
List (Hannover), die, im Wandel
Ostfriesland
Stade, Altes Land – Märchenstadt und Blütenmeer
Verden – der Landkreis

Nordrhein-Westfalen
Bergisch Gladbach – Schloss-Stadt an der Strunde

Baden-Württemberg
Freiburg im Breisgau
Konstanz schönste Seiten
Ludwigsburgs schönste Seiten

Bayern
Boten aus Stein – Alte Kirchen im Werdenfelser Land, am Staffelsee und im Ammergau
Garmisch-Partenkirchen – Herz des Werdenfelser Landes
Lüftlmalerei
Mittenwald, Krün, Wallgau

Unser Programm im Internet: **www.medien-verlag.de**